ALBUQUERQUE

Where the World Celebrates Ballooning

In association with

KODAK ALBUQUERQUE
INTERNATIONAL BALLOON FIESTA

STEVE YOUNG

DEDICATED TO:

The Founders and Original Pilots
Sid Cutter, Founder
Tom Rutherford, Founder

Bill Cutter, Gene Dennis, Denny Floden, Don Kerston, Bill Murtorff, Don Piccard, Wilma Piccard, Karl Stefan, Brent Stockwell, Carter Twedt, Matt Wiederkehr, Oscar Kratz

THANKS TO PAST PRESIDENTS:

Charlie Hines, Sherri Moore, Dick Rice, Bob Ruppenthal, Marge Ruppenthal, Gail Short, George Hahn, Jim Schumacher

Above: Reflected glory
Front cover: Small world FERNE SALTZMAN
Back cover: Mass animation FERNE SALTZMAN
Title page: Spirit of New Mexico Q13-KRQE TV

Prepared for Publication by American & World Geographic Publishing
Softbound ISBN 1-56037-113-7, Hardbound ISBN 1-56037-114-5

Greetings—

In the summer of 1972, I found myself aloft in a hot–air balloon, wondering how on earth I was going to land. It may not sound like much of a way to begin a love affair, yet that is perhaps the best description of what happened to me. I fell in love with the beauty and grace and simplicity of ballooning. Twenty–six years later, I'm still in love.

I could never have foreseen that ballooning would change my life. I certainly didn't foresee the effect it would have on me and on thousands of my neighbors in Albuquerque and New Mexico. Things started innocently enough, as more and more friends old and new embraced this novel form of flight. Ultimately, our passion led to the founding of the world's largest local ballooning organization and the world's largest ballooning event. I left the family business and started one of the world's largest private companies specializing in balloon operations and training.

FERNE SALTZMAN

Billowing pillow

Beyond this, ballooning gave a new identity to a city and a state. Not that long ago, if you went to another part of the United States and said you were from New Mexico, you were apt to be greeted with, "But your English is so good!" "Do you use pesos there?" "You can't mail this letter home without foreign postage." Nowadays, if you say you're from New Mexico—and more specifically, Albuquerque—the usual response is, "That's where they have all those balloons, isn't it?" People now know New Mexico is in the Union without looking at a map, and that's not a lot of hot air.

Ballooning in general, and the Kodak Albuquerque International Balloon Fiesta in particular, have touched more lives than I ever could have imagined. An often–visionary Board of Directors and thousands of volunteers have worked hard to make the Fiesta a world–renowned and world–class event. I am glad to have been a part of this team, and Albuquerque should be proud to be represented by them around the world.

The best is yet to come. The Balloon Fiesta's move in 1996 to a new and much larger launch site will make the 25th anniversary event the biggest ever held. Some 850 balloons are expected. Fifteen years ago, while dedicating another of the Fiesta's launch sites, I cheerfully predicted the Fiesta would grow to one thousand balloons. That day is coming soon, and I can hardly wait.

This book will give you a sense of the pageantry, color, and fun of the world's biggest balloon rally. While it cannot capture the whole experience—the roar of the burners, the smell of Indian fry bread wafting across the field, the cheering crowd—it is the next best thing to being there, in the skies above Albuquerque, in October. Welcome aboard, and enjoy the flight!

Soft landings,

Sid Cutter

Above: Traffic jammin'

FERNE SALTZMAN

All keyed up

EVERY OCTOBER, JUST ABOUT THE TIME THE LEAVES BEGIN TO TURN TO GOLD atop the Sandia Mountains and the nip of fall chills the air in the Rio Grande Valley below, hundreds of thousands of people descend on Albuquerque to watch balloons ascend into the clear New Mexico sky.

This nine–day orgy of sound and color is the Kodak Albuquerque International Balloon Fiesta. Its sheer size boggles the mind. A small staff and an army of volunteers in the thousands orchestrate more than 850 balloons and one thousand pilots who fly the massive mass ascensions, competitions, separate exhibitions of "special shape" and gas balloons, and the nighttime displays known as "balloon glows." As the millennium approaches, the Fiesta is not only the world's biggest balloon rally, it is the world's most photographed event.

As one looks at the Fiesta today, it's hard to remember that until June of 1971 there were *no* balloons in Albuquerque. Balloon flights were not completely unknown, of course. The first, piloted by one Park VanTassel, ascended in 1882. Through the next eighty years occasional adventurers brought in balloons for exhibitions, but ballooning on a large scale awaited the invention of the modern hot–air balloon in the 1950's. The sport grew slowly through the sixties, but balloons were still rare and exotic objects.

Albuquerque's first resident balloon was intended not for aviation, but for decoration. Sid Cutter, faced with converting an entire hanger into a party room with a World War I theme, somehow came up with the idea of putting a balloon in the cavernous space. After all, they used balloons for reconnaissance in World War I, and balloons

FERNE SALTZMAN

Phantom pilots; phantom crews

were big enough to pack a lot of decorating punch. So Cutter had a balloon built in patriotic red, white, and blue and stuffed the six–story concoction into the hanger. He never had any intention of flying it—"it looked like a very dangerous aviation vehicle to me," he commented—but his brother Bill and his friends wouldn't let him off so lightly. When Cutter inflated the balloon the next day, intending simply to run it up and down on a tether and give a few rides, they untied the rope!

This first flight was a somewhat unnerving experience, but by the time it ended the Cutter brothers were hooked. Sid Cutter took to flying the balloon around town, and wherever it flew it attracted entranced onlookers. By November 1971 he had enough converts to form a club, the Albuquerque Aerostat Ascension Association, which today is the world's largest local ballooning organization. And by the next April, Cutter and the fledgling balloon club had taken KOB Radio's idea for a 50th anniversary promotion and turned it into the "Albuquerque Roadrunner–Coyote Balloon Race." Bad weather in the Midwest and shipping problems prevented the rally from becoming the world's biggest, as Cutter and KOB had hoped. Still, 14 balloons flew in what eventually became known as the "first Fiesta." Sixty–five thousand awestruck spectators crowded onto a vacant lot that is now part of Coronado Center. The balloonists themselves were stunned by the crowd's reaction. Don Kersten, then the president of the Balloon Federation of America, was so impressed that he offered to bring the first World Hot Air Ballooning Championships to Albuquerque. Cutter and the city accepted the offer that sealed the city's position as the "ballooning capital of the world."

The First World Championships were held in February 1973 at the State Fairgrounds. Fully a quarter of the world's hot–air balloons (138) were on hand. The incredible publicity generated by the event supported a period of explosive growth in the ballooning community worldwide and in Albuquerque in particular. The third Fiesta, even without a major competition attached, had nearly as many balloons as the Worlds the previous year. By the time of the Second World Championships in 1975, the total had climbed to 168, forcing the Fiesta to make the first of many physical relocations. It left the fairgrounds for land loaned by the Simms Family southwest of Osuna Road and I–25, and moved from February to October to take advantage of better weather.

In that year the Fiesta also began its metamorphosis from private enterprise to community event. The event had become too big and costly for Sid Cutter's private company, World Balloon Championships (now World Balloon Corporation) to handle on its own. With the support of then–Albuquerque mayor Harry Kinney, Cutter turned the operation over to a private, non–profit corporation, Albuquerque International Balloon Fiesta, Inc. One of the first decisions made was to de–emphasize serious international competition. Although competitive events always remained as a part of Fiesta, the emphasis (which remains today) would be on "fun" flying and on sharing the sport with spectators.

FERNE SALTZMAN

Sunburst over basket

Through the next several years the growth of the Fiesta was paralleled by the growth of the local ballooning community. Each Fiesta brought new converts to the sport, and the enthusiastic volunteer support provided by those converts allowed the Fiesta to grow and become an increasingly diverse event. Simultaneously, the fame of some Albuquerque balloonists ascended to stratospheric heights through an impressive series of competitive successes and record flights. Sid Cutter became National Hot Air Balloon Champion in 1978 and 1986, and Paul Woessner won world hot–air ballooning titles in 1977 and 1979. The first National Hot Air Team Championship was won in 1995 by Cutter, Mark Sullivan, and Troy Bradley. Carol Rymer Davis, Sue Hazlett, and Connie March all set world altitude records. In 1978, the late Ben Abruzzo, the late Maxie Anderson, and Larry Newman set the world on its ear when they completed the first successful transatlantic crossing by balloon in the *Double Eagle II*. All three men then added to their laurels with an incredible series of "firsts." Maxie and Kris Anderson successfully crossed the North American continent non–stop in 1980. Abruzzo, Newman, Ron Clark, and Rocky Aoki's epic *Double Eagle V* trans–Pacific flight in 1981 is a feat that went unduplicated for more than ten years. As recently as 1992, Troy Bradley and Richard Abruzzo broke the *Double Eagle II*'s duration record during a transatlantic flight. Ben Abruzzo (1984), Richard Abruzzo (1994), and Mark Sullivan (1995) have all won the National Gas Balloon Championship.

By the early 1980's the Fiesta had moved north to Cutter Field, between Paseo Del Norte and Osuna Road. Besides balloon ascensions the event now included parachute jumpers, aerobatic exhibitions, radio–controlled aircraft, equestrian demonstrations, high school bands, ultralites, model balloons, and a dizzying number of social functions. Gas balloons were exhibited at the Fiesta in the late '70's, and in 1981 a gas balloon race became part of the Fiesta's regular lineup. The Key Grab, where bal-

STEVE YOUNG

Mass exhilaration

loonists fly to the field and snatch the keys to a car from the top of a pole, became an annual institution from the moment of its inception in 1978.

In 1986 the event was on the move again, to Balloon Fiesta Park just south of Alameda Boulevard, and in 1996 it moved north to its present site. The spectacular nighttime balloon display known as the "Balloon Glow" was added in 1987 to honor the 75th anniversary of New Mexico statehood. It was an immediate hit and quickly became a permanent part of the Fiesta. The first Special Shapes Rodeo was held in 1989, and the enormous popularity of these incredibly engineered, fantastic creations has resulted in a steady expansion of "special shape" events.

After a quarter of a century of operation, the Kodak Albuquerque International Balloon Fiesta has matured into one of the nation's premier community festivals. It has become as synonymous with Albuquerque as the Kentucky Derby is with Louisville, the Rose Bowl with Pasadena, or the Indy 500 with Indianapolis. The breathtaking sight of hundreds of ascending balloons punctuated with the excited cries of children and the roar of balloon burners has lured thousands to those dusty fields north of Albuquerque. The incredible warmth of the balloonists and volunteers who are so willing to share their passion for the sport, and the unparalleled hospitality of the city of Albuquerque, has kept them coming back. This book is a visual testament to a love and commitment that has brought so much joy to so many people.

Facing page: Soar, Dino, soar STEVE YOUNG

Right: Modern art minus canvas

Below: Packin' it in

STEVE YOUNG

STEVE YOUNG

Christmas tree ornaments affixed to sky

STEVE YOUNG

Slow burn with incandescent rhythms

FERNE SALTZMAN

Wanna hear an **eeegal** *joke?*

FERNE SALTZMAN

The ears have it

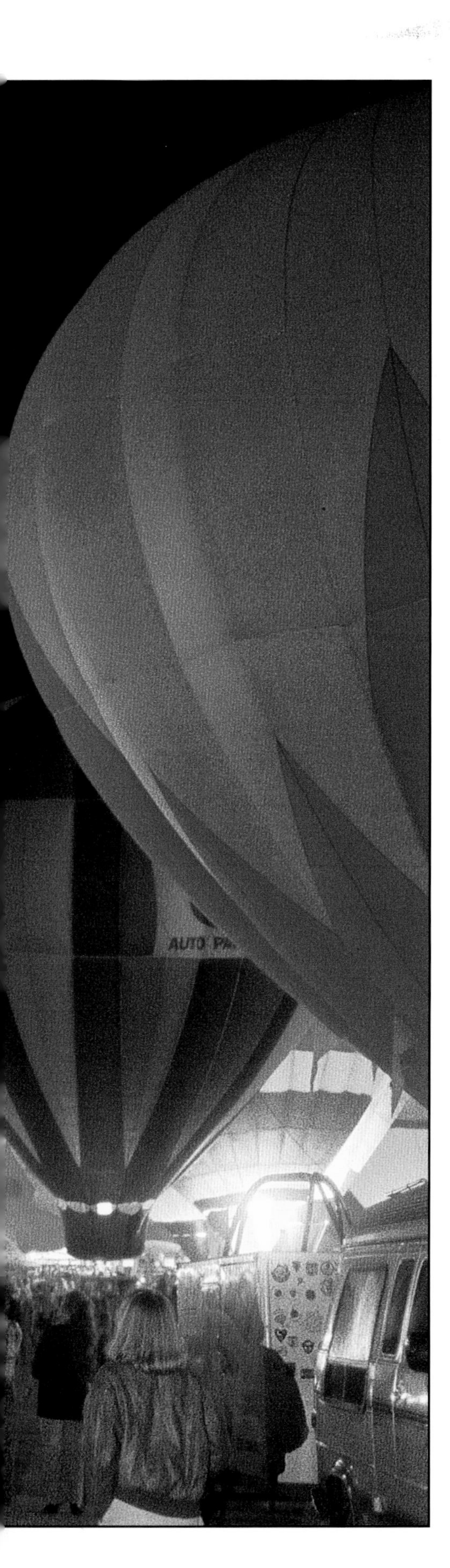

Right: Debonair polar bear

Below: Balloon enthusiasts' paradise

Facing page: Basket encircled by bright surround sound STEVE YOUNG

STEVE YOUNG

STEVE YOUNG

LAKES, CA

Big belly ballet

STEVE YOUNG

STEVE YOUNG

Splash & Dash: Wet, wild, wonderful!

Blast off! Lift off! Launch!

STEVE YOUNG

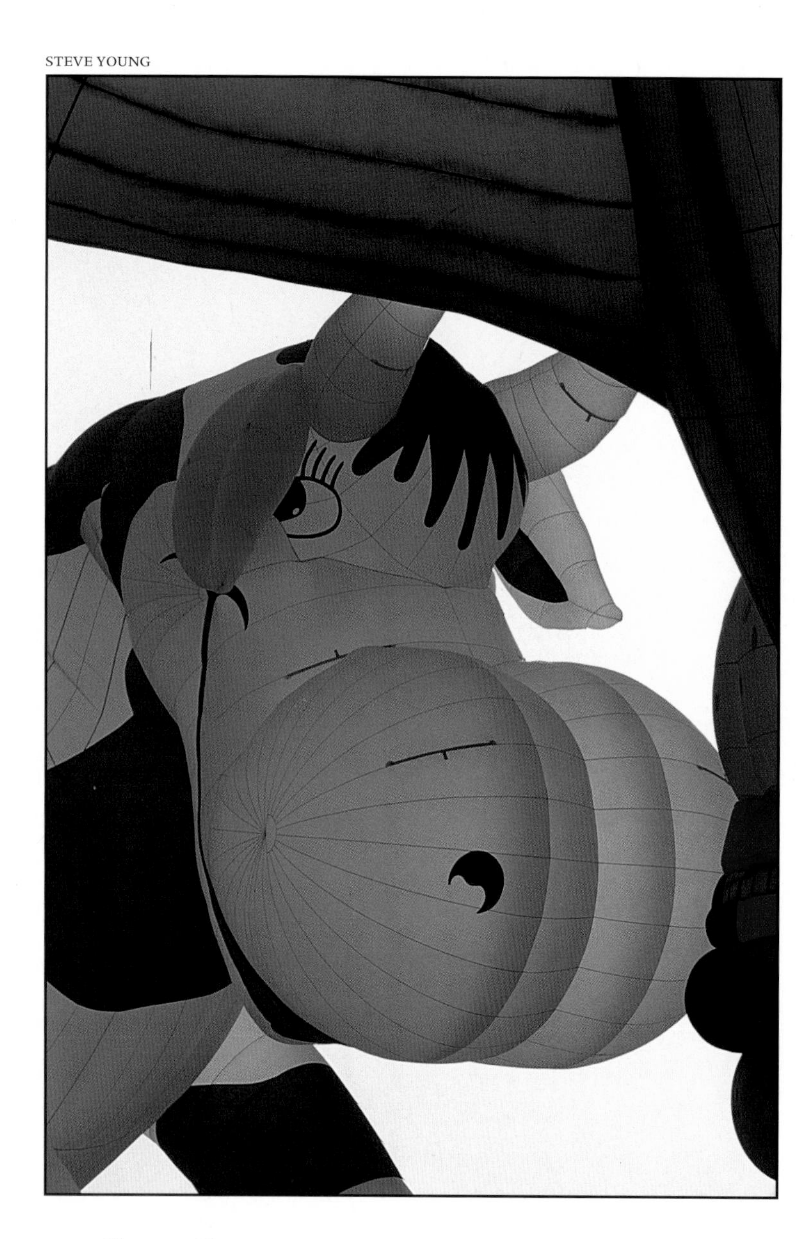

Above: Charismatic cow

Right: Curtain rising on second-act.

STEVE YOUNG

FERNE SALTZMAN

Above: Centered pinwheel

Right: Wanna ride on the Dragon Wagon?

STEVE YOUNG

Sterling serenity

FERNE SALTZMAN

Fiery dreamstuff

STEVE YOUNG

Left: Happiness: A Fiesta trademark

Below: Predictable pandemonium

FERNE SALTZMAN

Ripstop pop

STEVE YOUNG

Flags 'n' bags

STEVE YOUNG

Gordon Bennett gas-a-thonic experience

STEVE YOUNG

Potential pinwheel

STEVE YOUNG

I'd like to put some real teeth in your spokes.

FERNE SALTZMAN

Fire in the belly

STEVE YOUNG

Mixed shades and shadows

FERNE SALTZMAN

Windsong melodies

Right: Inside. Outside. Topside. Underside.

Below: Octagons of Tiffany glass

FERNE SALTZMAN

FERNE SALTZMAN

FERNE SALTZMAN

Tethered menagerie

STEVE YOUNG

Above: Suleyman & friends—much, much larger than life

Right: Count the colors of Mass Ascension

STEVE YOUNG

STEVE YOUNG

Above: Flamenco colors expand

Facing page: Mr. Frank needs pickle, relish, & ketchup on the side. STEVE YOUNG

STEVE YOUNG

STEVE YOUNG

Above: Walking through a red ripstop landscape

Right: Peacock preening for cameras

STEVE YOUNG

A bevy. A bewilderment. A blessing. . . of balloons

STEVE YOUNG

Santa Maria at full sail

FERNE SALTZMAN

Canopy of spirals

STEVE YOUNG

In your ear, Mr. Pilot.

Right: Balloon bouquet
Below: Field in bloom

STEVE YOUNG

STEVE YOUNG

STEVE YOUNG

I've lost my floss!

FERNE SALTZMAN

Blue-ribbon ride

FERNE SALTZMAN

Left: Felix the Cat

Below: Leaning Tower of Eagle

FERNE SALTZMAN

FERNE SALTZMAN

Above: Charged-up zebra

Right: Balloons over blazing horizon

JEAN MICHEL BERTRAND

Sandbar splashdown

STEVE YOUNG

Ladder of 3-D stripes

FERNE SALTZMAN

Cow-a-bonga!

FERNE SALTZMAN

Right: Why don't we stay here forever?

Below: Egg-statically yolking it up

Facing page: Inverse stripes

FERNE SALTZMAN

FERNE SALTZMAN

FERNE SALTZMAN

Balloon bouquet

Facing page: Star-spangled symbol FERNE SALTZMAN

FERNE SALTZMAN

Right: Foil-wrapped candy drops

Below: Who says I need a pedicure?

FERNE SALTZMAN

STEVE YOUNG

Technicolor trio

Study in zodiac blue

FERNE SALTZMAN

Left: No-melt snowman

Below: Scene of drifting dreams

STEVE YOUNG

STEVE YOUNG

Above: High altitude hi-five

Right: Tony Tiger smiling brightly/Looming large & very spritely

STEVE YOUNG

FERNE SALTZMAN

Gondola gondoliers

FERNE SALTZMAN

Q-13/KRQE TV

Above: I think I'm in love.

Left: Spirit of New Mexico

STEVE YOUNG

View from a tent flap

Facing page: The first wave STEVE YOUNG

Kentucky
Fried Chicken

All fired up

STEVE YOUNG

Gourmet mushrooms

STEVE YOUNG

Initiation, right?

FERNE SALTZMAN

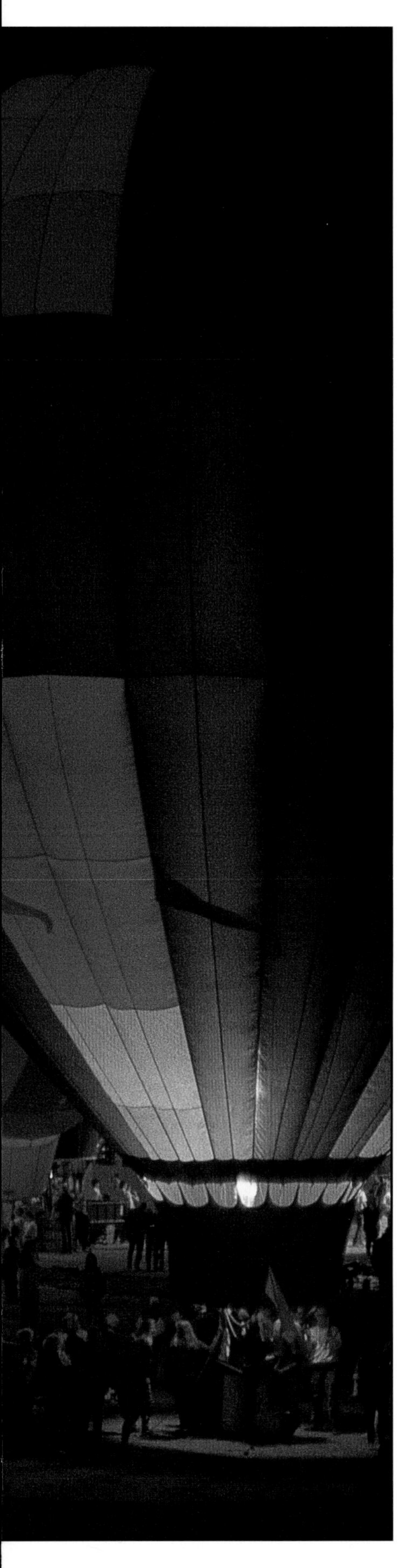

JEAN MICHEL BERTRAND

Above: Sandbags set with measured steps

Left: The glow show

N2622D

STEVE YOUNG

Left: Dancing dinosaur

Below: Let's all land right there!

Facing page: Powder puff polka STEVE YOUNG

STEVE YOUNG

FERNE SALTZMAN

Bedouin tent perspective

FERNE SALTZMAN

Left: Patchwork prints

Below: Solo shadow

FERNE SALTZMAN

FERNE SALTZMAN

FERNE SALTZMAN

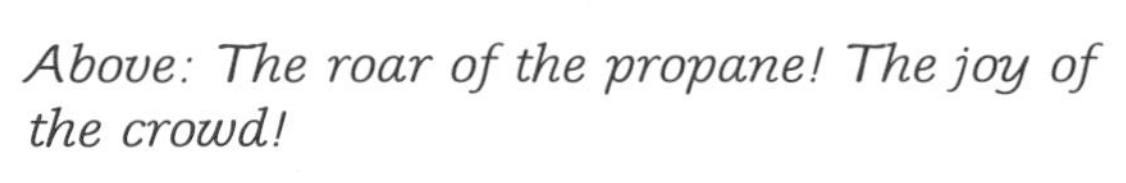

Above: The roar of the propane! The joy of the crowd!

Left: Harley revving for the skyway

STEVE YOUNG

STEVE YOUNG

Above: Miss Piggy in reverse

Right: Field performers create impromptu routines

Facing page: When balloons land on sand, getting wet's no sweat. STEVE YOUNG

Morning glory

STEVE YOUNG

Sailing through silvered sky-space

FERNE SALTZMAN

FERNE SALTZMAN

Above: Crayola playola

Right: Coloration situation

STEVE YOUNG

Eyes of Egypt

STEVE YOUNG

Yellow sub with air capability

FERNE SALTZMAN

STEVE YOUNG

Above: Starstruck

Left: Risin' with the sun

G-BUW
-WYCH

STEVE YOUNG

Sighting of carrot-billed stork

Facing page: Ark on air STEVE YOUNG

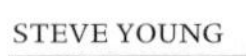
STEVE YOUNG

Parasol parade

SIZZLER
76

STEVE YOUNG

Beauty squared

Facing page: Balloon boogie on the bar STEVE YOUNG

FERNE SALTZMAN

Spontaneous sky deco

STEVE YOUNG

Vermilion & crushed velvet

STEVE YOUNG

Amphibious basket

I fly like an real eagle, but I bet that bear needs sonar.

STEVE YOUNG

Above: Mickey's dream castle

Left: Cumulus colors

Dawn touchdown

STEVE YOUNG

Key Grab

Suspended candy dish

STEVE YOUNG

Riveted audience

STEVE YOUNG

Left: Clown playin' footsie

Below: Stealing a kiss

FERNE SALTZMAN

Small world

FERNE SALTZMAN

Flat-bottomed wicker boat

STEVE YOUNG

The Liberty bird is on the ring.

FERNE SALTZMAN

A crunch of dreams makes a gourmet brunch.

STEVE YOUNG

Undulating collage

A box of candy to sweeten the morning

STEVE YOUNG

STEVE YOUNG

A cluster of canopies

STEVE YOUNG

Conflagration congregation

STEVE YOUNG

The nose knows

D-OCFT
Warsteiner

STEVE YOUNG

Air anemone

Facing page: Spectacle at sunset STEVE YOUNG

Wearing a crown of darts and stars

FERNE SALTZMAN

Crowd control is my bag!

FERNE SALTZMAN

Humpty Dumpty off the wall—last seen scrambling to Nepal.

STEVE YOUNG

World-wide pennant display

STEVE YOUNG

Predator afloat: Stingray rising

STEVE YOUNG

Right Watch out, Saguaro; it's cactus salad time.

Below: Fabric Popsicle flavors

Facing page: Daylight stars

FERNE SALTZMAN

FERNE SALTZMAN

Comet
CLEANS ALBUQUERQUE
KODAK

STEVE YOUNG

FERNE SALTZMAN

Above: Not hot dog—top dog.

Left: A lift of spirits

FERNE SALTZMAN

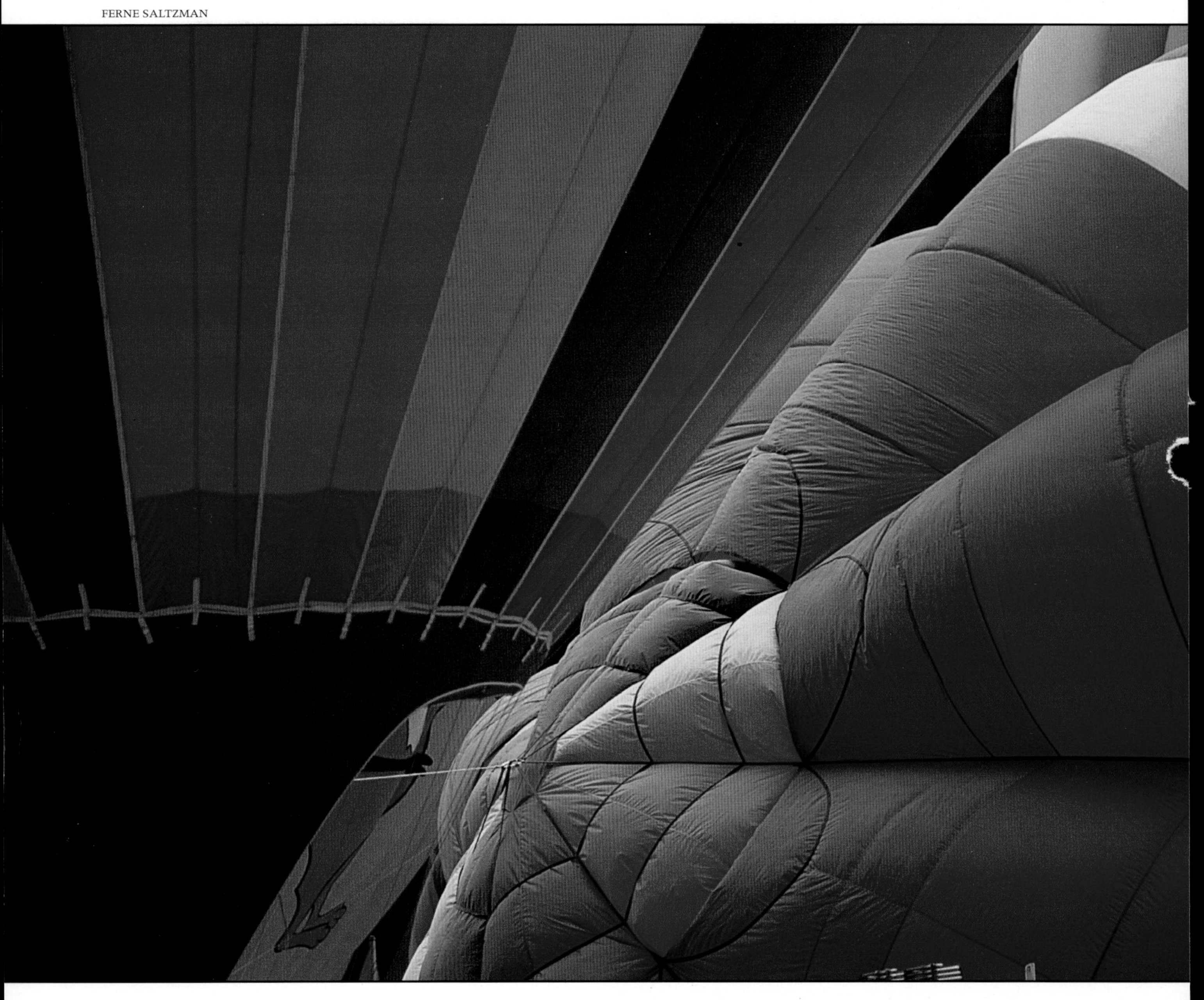

Quilted symmetry

Gas balloon challenging darkness FERNE SALTZMAN

Bright & breathtaking launch

KODAK ALBUQUERQUE INTERNATIONAL BALLOON FIESTA
"Where The World Celebrates Ballooning"
1996 Board Members & Staff

Officers:

Bruce Hale, President
Mark Sullivan, Vice President
John R. Sena, Treasurer
Cookie M. See, Secretary

Board Members:

Richard Abruzzo
Sam H. Baxter
Pat Brake
Dick Butterfield
Ron Caldwell
Neida L. Courtney
John C. Davis IV
Jacqueline Hockey
Steven A. Komadina, M.D.
Rodney A. May
Tom S. McConnell, M.D.
Frank A. Mezzancello
Robert O. Moore
Anna Nalley
Judy E. Roberts
Harry T. Season, Jr.
Jim Shiver
Steven M. Shope
Arthur J. Swenka
Al Tetreault

Staff:

Sam J. Hancock, Executive Director
Jodi Baugh, Marketing/Communications Director
Jim "Badtoe" Benson, Field Manager
Sandy Bertola, Concessions/Special
Shapes Rodeo Event Coordinator
Linda A. Forsythe, Pilot Coordinator
Donna Gober, Bookkeeper
Carolyn Pica, Receptionist
Brett Schuler, Marketing Assistant